"*Have You Been Long Enough at Table* is both a question and an invitation in Leslie Sainz's marvelous debut. Sainz probes spirituality with the verve and vitality of Emily Dickinson if Dickinson had been born Cuban American at the end of the last century. Sainz probes the overlap of imagination and experience like Sylvia Plath if Plath was born to a Cuban American landscape between 'field crickets, memory, [and] lesser parasites.' *Have You Been Long Enough at Table* articulates the bonds and tensions of independence and tradition, spirit and form, home and exile. The narratives ring with the integrity of memoir and the inventiveness of allegory. Nature, politics, and humor overlap in an image where 'The Black Wasps wear green berets.' Story is transformed into spell, chant, beat: 'Mothers, wives, sisters, daughters radiating as verbs under a mahogany roof.' These lyrics of 'the land—much in us still' are classic and altogether new. Leslie Sainz is a poet who has been long at the table reading and writing poems and long at the table listening to the poetry of culture and family. She makes questions invitations and memory visible. Come bear witness to a remarkable poet bearing witness."

—TERRANCE HAYES,
author of *American Sonnets for
My Past and Future Assassin*

"The music in this book is able to combine not just melody but also emotion. The emotion here isn't just heart but also a thoughtful exploration. The thought here isn't just ideas but a deepening journey. There is much to love in *Have You Been Long Enough at Table*—but most of all I love its variousness; that's music itself."

—ILYA KAMINSKY,
author of *Deaf Republic*

"From sonnets for deities to poems for mothers, women, and family, this collection exists beautifully at the intersection of mythology and history, both personal and political. Just like its title, this book asks questions that resist simple answers, all the while giving us moments of tenderness, like this one: 'The orchids are lovely / this time of year / and the women, writing.'"

—ZEINA HASHEM BECK,
author of *O*

"Sainz's debut poetry collection is a triumph, deftly capturing vivid images of displacement, and transcending borders and language. Cuba is the pounding heart of these poems."

—RICHARD BLANCO,
author of *How to Love a Country*

HAVE YOU BEEN LONG ENOUGH AT TABLE

HAVE YOU BEEN
LONG ENOUGH
AT TABLE

POEMS

LESLIE SAINZ

TIN HOUSE / PORTLAND, OREGON

First US Edition 2023
Printed in the United States of America

Jean Valentine, excerpt from "(Two were seen leaving)" from *Break the Glass*.
Copyright © 2010 by Jean Valentine. Reprinted with the permission of The Permissions
Company, LLC on behalf of Copper Canyon Press, coppercanyonpress.org.

Manufacturing by Kingery Printing Company
Interior design by Beth Steidle

Library of Congress Cataloging-in-Publication Data

Names: Sainz, Leslie, 1992– author.
Title: Have you been long enough at table : poems / Leslie Sainz.
Description: Portland, Oregon : Tin House, 2023.
Identifiers: LCCN 2023019924 | ISBN 9781959030119 (paperback) |
ISBN 9781959030195 (ebook)
Subjects: LCSH: Cuban Americans—Poetry. | LCGFT: Poetry.
Classification: LCC PS3619.A3985 H38 2023 | DDC 811/.6—dc23/eng/20230503
LC record available at https://lccn.loc.gov/2023019924

Tin House
2617 NW Thurman Street, Portland, OR 97210
www.tinhouse.com

DISTRIBUTED BY W. W. NORTON & COMPANY

1 2 3 4 5 6 7 8 9 0

Para mis padres

TABLE OF CONTENTS

iii

HAVE YOU BEEN LONG ENOUGH AT TABLE

"El vino, de plátano; y si sale agrio, ¡es nuestro vino!"
—JOSÉ MARTÍ

"but not hunger

or hunger not granted"
—JEAN VALENTINE

ÑO

Para los balseros

There is no country

where the dead don't float.

Men and children going,

having gone,   lungwet

across thickened water.

Be it the body to know

what's missing. To call

back the colors. At sea

the stomach is a bugle

though I've heard it

called a scream.

Oil drums headless

as monarchs, styrofoam

on the knees. Said of

regimes: under or over.

Here or there.

The orchids are lovely

this time of year

and the women, writing.

What covers the land

and is the land—

much in us still.

i

SONNET FOR ELEGUÁ

In pursuit of an ending, I quickened my pace. I had no questions,

not my own, to recover in. The only certainty: the evening

under the oil palm when you gave me my dry feet.

From then on, dreams as warm as atoms. The exiled boy, always

desperate to be heard, appeared mostly as crickets and hinges.

Three summers ago, he mutilated a pigeon by hurling it

against the wall of the market. It made sounds like the latch

rattle of an icebox and the stain never came out, even

when we used aguardiente. I've left my outline in worse

places. Lately, by the window, where I count the women

with thicker, blacker hair, study the way it tightens around

their shoulders like bulls ascending. What occupies me

is also running. It never tires, but rather, repositions itself.

I should like to reposition myself, please. All of me this time.

NOTICE TO APPEAR

It goes doorbell
(two beats)
then knocking
(three or more beats)
or knocking
(five beats)
then doorbell (three times,
two beats each).
The very first beat disappears
the front door.
We abrupt.
We.
Any way possible, silence.
Beat beat
then beat beat beat beat.
We crawl to Mother
and Father's closet
staying close
to the grout.
Together we have
four pairs of legs.
I am short and young
enough already
not to be seen
and Brother is taller and
growing. Beat beat beat
beat beat beat beat
beat beat beat beat.
Our hearts (four)
are summoned into this
beating, so the sound of

heavy listening
(Mother heavy listens best).
Our hearts (four) are so
impressionable, our ears
(eight) are so airless
and impressionable.
Beat beat.
In the closet we crouch
on top of each other
(Father's disappearance
that close) and look
like more legs.
Beat beat
beat beat
beat.
The house black and whites.
Brother and I heavy
listen to Mother looking at Father
as though he is
her husband only.
Our impressionable hearts
(two),
our airless ears
(four).
Beat
beat
beat
beat
beat
beat
beat
beat
beat
beat

beat.
On the property's
perimeter,
legs
(two)
with large feet in boots
on the patio.
That sound.
That close.

I am still underground when I hear that the ALLIGATOR MAN is dead,
belly-up, awaiting the furnace. Father delivers the news
along with my daily rations, his hands dutiful, nurse-like.
Bicho malo nunca muere, he says, dropping the rope into the well.
I know this to mean: *Do not celebrate. There is little difference
between being followed and being haunted.*

> With each passing hour I learn more about chance and limits.
> I learn that the earth has a jaw too, swallows at will like a man.
> When I was younger, I thought only the ocean could make things
> disappear: a raft, a family. I now suspect everything takes orders
> from somewhere.

There are lots of dead rats in the well, but one is fatter than the others.
He has a large red gash on his forehead that looks like a salute, so I name him
EL COMANDANTE. In the well, I'm the one who gives speeches.
I prop EL COMANDANTE into a kneel and talk at length about legacy, how easy it is
for a tide to erase decades of work in the sand. Less than a mile away,
the wild applause of metal on metal. When I finish my speech I take a bow.

> Mother visits at night and speaks of rescue. She says the men meant to
> liberate me are organizing the best they can, that they still need time.
> I lie down in the black water and think about history. My blood
> so patient. My back so wet there's a name for it.

Near-prayer and not. Pink, red flowers, orange and yellow
flowers and white. In this very moment, for different reasons,
this is as specific as I can be in both languages.
Day of the Holy Cross—she dies, femininely,
on Día de la Cruz. Exactly who performs the miracle?
The dead and buried son shimmies to his mother's
dead and buried breast to suckle. Miracle. Thinking of
Archimedes's bathwater, the Cuban sculptor gives her
density, porelessness, in 20th-century Carrara. Exactly.
It is true statues are cruel when they're accurate. It is
still true that statues are cruel when they're not. On the edge
of my cowardice, reason. Who exactly could call me
by name in that cemetery? Gladiolus, ginger, lilies. Young
women are a series of images. We are regimes.

SUNDAY, WOUNDED

Para las Damas de Blanco

Mothers, wives, sisters, daughters radiating
as verbs under a mahogany roof.

Radiating as angels.

The imprisoned are

now

but not *here*.

Just there, orders in the gumlines
of the men on the sidewalk.

Mass finishes.

The women feed their missing
to the church walls,

the women derange the street with their dead.

¡Libertad! ¡Libertad! ¡Libertad!

They link hands and birth a prism.

The men open their fists like cylinders.

¡Libertad!

¡Libertad!

¡Libertad!

Blows, howls. Flesh

folding into itself like a sheet—
white, reddened.

Mothers, wives, sisters, daughters followed,

surveilled,

clicks on their phone lines
like snapping in a nearby dream.

The tongueless republic,

unable to lick its wounds,

does not sleep.

CLIMATE FEEDBACK

Say how can you leave with a sea that tall

O say can you leave

Can the sea

That's all

Say you leave that

How

With what

Is that all

Say you can

Say the sea

Say it leaves you et al

Can you see that at all

O you can

After all

After sea

After leave

It does leave after all

Can you say

Can you see

How it sees you

In all

How it says what it sees

What it needs

How that's all

How that's all you can do

You can say

All in all

When the sea makes you leave

Makes you leave

In its all

Can you see it

In your leaving

Can you even leave

At all

With a wave

With another

And another

Et al

APOSTLE

There's the fast-eating river, green
and hiccupping. If it could
brush against mine, your arm,
a little less dead. In an afterlife,
(yours or mine?)
fish stagnant as earlobes.

.

Metaphorical bells around
your neck and shoulders
(we are so bombarded by sound.)
Amor cuerdo, no es amor,
something an apostle might say.
Your forehead, nose, mustache—
they unify your face
like a strong agreement.
Have I felt, ever, strong
like two men, at least two?
Who would allow that?

.

Devotion, loyalty, they are
slippery and slow. They are terrible
rivers. I am making a point, I hope,
when I drown my independence
(red, dark, blue)
within earshot of the living.

MIGUELITO / MARIELITO

The leading man does not know us as we know us.
He does not consider what we could do
for him, for his country.

The fan, warped, blasts and rickets. The television moves
its Soviet hips. I raise an index finger to my mouth
when Miguelito's crying gets loud,

though it makes my face an officer.
The government asked him to paint propaganda—
large fists eclipsed by stars,

the many machine guns of EL COMANDANTE—
and he told them he would rather fuck his boyfriend.

They won't come for him until he's sleeping.

I try to raise the volume and the glow of the television turns
blue. Miguelito presses his forehead against the screen
as if to fuse into it, but US does not enter us.

All along the street, varying degrees of dimming.
Everyone we know ends the day this way, making
lifelines of their eyes.

Decades later, when an American asks him to speak
on the role of forgiveness in his work, he'll say,

It takes years and years and years. And then it takes a lifetime.

GLASSWARE

I

Overhearing an argument, something beneath
my cheeks like heat, like cowbells.
I am at my most probable, most liquid,
suddenly. I come when called.

II

Over dinner, a man, melting, sells American pillows
through the television. The napkins are of a thick paper.
The dishware, all rounded, the color of most bandages.
I am impressed by my convincing father and loyal mother.
Their face veins make clear they are not lying to themselves,
not themselves. Faithfully, I am a large shard
made of their smaller shards. If you were to
turn my ears inside out: hot skin, sleep, *only trust your family.*

III

My father used to blow glass in California, sell plated jewelry
from a dark grey suitcase, have regrets. My mother worked
for Eastern Air Lines and ate very little. Now, my mother lives
alone and with my father in Miami. My father lives
with my mother and, some days, himself.

IV

When I am hurt, my sorry skull vibrates, needs sleep.
I was barefoot when glass appeared on the floor.
This time, most times, rage to keep it company.
When no one apologizes, my eyes roll
out of my head as packets of fake sugar.

V

Shortly after the Revolution, children, students, worked
the sugarcane fields. I hear this because it is
told to me in the kitchen by my hurt parents.
In 1964, a 12-year-old boy named Arnaldo Garrillo was said
to have cut 7,608 pounds of cane a day.
FIDEL holds still the record: 9,230 pounds.

VI

Sugar appears in many American fantasies.
The convincing '60s sugar glass made to simulate
broken windows and windshields? I will never taste it.
It doesn't harm the actor, it harms the actor, argues
the Internet. Transparent, brittle sugar.
When I study the '60s, other time periods, my eyes turn red
like from cameras, or rum, or furnaces, or sand.

LEFT ARM / RIGHT ARM

Veins are not worms, rivers, branches. They are maggots.
/
When your country says give, you drain despite the clots.

SIERRA DEL ESCAMBRAY

Loud, verdant. The musculature of hanging
palm, sugar-air damp on the shoulders.

Toco-toco-tocoro-tocoro
a trogon sings in even cuts of yarn.

El guía says *red belly, white throat.*
El guía says *they nest in what's left over.*

The sun behind the clouds twitches like a goat tail.

I have the dream about helicopters,
about symmetry—heads

not unlike mine split down the middle
as if for sharing.

Los rebeldes said *look* when they meant *listen.*
Los rebeldes crouched at the waters fall,
            tombstone-high.

Now, in the off-season, men and women
with pink hands, backpacks.

El guía shoos a foraging pig
to widen the path, or

the same sun choking.

What have you been offered? What did you take?

GUSANO (N):

1. WORM
2. SLUR FOR CUBAN EXILES

In need   of handling.
    Gusanos.   *Capitalistas.*
Chafing   a bowl   of sky,
the plane's   rudder like
a   spatula.   Three
    young sons,   their father,   the
littlest   mother,   feeling   scraped.
Escoria.   *Mafiosos.*
       Sleeping,   waking,
my   father,   the   defector.
   Flight time: three   and
a half   hours   only.
Abuelita   remembers,   fondly,
 the hospitals,   the milkmen's
uniforms.   A   year
later,   from   a city   dubbed
                    Prisontown,
Abuelito   addresses   FIDEL
          via   telegram:
Feliz Cumpleaños.
     I hope you never have another.
   FIDEL responds:
Come back to Cuba,   and we'll talk.

1959.   My   mother   is
the   height   of six
          stacked   corpses   when
she is   smuggled

onto a Pan Am flight   to
        Jamaica.
Her tears   are   headless.
       From her hair   her sisters
pluck: continuity,   their mother's
   voice,   several violets.
        Privilegiado.
On arrival,   a priest
delivers   the young girls   to
a   convent.
     They   live.   And   go
   to school.
Field   crickets,   memory,   lesser
       parasites.
My   mother   takes
      her first steps   into
   the arms   of a   nun.
200 miles north,   men shuffle
into lines   against   el paredón.

OPERATION GOOD TIMES

It would/could reflect poorly on the regime if this were to
get out   If this were to get out the way the poor would
get   Out on the regime could you reflect on getting out
of the regime if you would/could reflect on this if this
reflected the way out if this were one   Would this reflect
poorly this poorly this regime   It would   Could it get
out of this were this to get out   It could   This could
get out if this reflected on/out reflected out poorly
     Could it get poorer   It would   Poor on the way
out   Pour out the regime   The regime to get out
poorly to get on/out the out the out get out get out get
out get on go on get out

CONJUGATE / DEMONSTRATE

I am trying to get this right.
You are still so trusting.
She is ashamed.
He is inescapable.
They are unaware of me.
We are our own beds.

I am not the fluent speaker.
You are not disarmed yet.
She is not altogether Un-American.
He is not escapable.
They are not their statesmen.
We are not yet exhausted.

I was living here-there.
You were looking to me for answers.
She was.
He was a dictator.
They were exercising a right.
We were supposed to do something.

I was not prepared for my own harm.
You were not prepared for your own harm.
She was not altogether American.
He was ~~not~~ just here somewhere.
They were not seen again.
We were not supposed to do that.

I have been and
You have been disarmed.
She has been outlanded.
He has been eulogized.
They have been so patient.
We have been at fault.

I have not been.
You have not been a little scared?
She has not stepped foot on the island.
He has not been laid to rest.
They have not been given hope.
We have not been forgiven.

SONNET FOR SHANGO

The woman who raised the woman who raised me was a mistress.

She met her lover at the tops of trees, screamed so loud

her tongue shoveled the sky. I don't ask for as much.

I know there are better silences than my face in my hands,

you at your nearest. Still, hold me as a king would.

Madden me. They did not name me María

because even as an infant it was clear I could not abstain.

Before striking a neighboring town, lightning looks

both ways. December falls like sheet music,

like eyelashes, and again men sharpen themselves

in your name. Bastion. Frenzy. The same blood spilling.

Before you leave, I store half of me in the batea and the rest

at the nape of your neck. Fire, each of your fingers—

there is nothing more generous, more just.

STILL LIFE WITH CHRIST, AROMATICS

The night, good, is a gorgeous clone of itself.
Thinking of the slick roaches
defecating in the silverware trays? Three times only.
In two stacked plastic bags, five sour oranges pecking
like past selves. The baroque
garlic. The one and a half small onions.
I squint at the tip of my nose until it becomes Abuelita's. Gorgeous,
good night with salt pork, cumin, oregano. Salt in the machacador,
softening. Poinsettias court the window, court the light.
Accidentally, inevitably, I leave some skin cells while retrieving four bay leaves.
Never, ever, salt the beans says the father whose
stiff fingers cannot shatter
the cooking wine bottle because it is plastic.
At midnight, the hair on my shoulder is someone else's.

MAL DE OJO

I study her hip bones, midday.
Something crackles through the trees—no, a withering.

I let the last malanga rot on the counter because it is easier
not to have to cut another thing open.

Bulls in my blood, pawing. The winter of it all.

Days later, I make another woman my enemy.
I follow her for three blocks before I trip over my envy,

forget to lessen myself. When I hit the sidewalk,
I feel my mother fall in Florida, and her mother, the same.

But I am smaller now than I was then.
Please, do not ask about my thens.

SONNET FOR YEMAYÁ

When will heaven happen? Will heaven happen?

I was not there, I was there, hovering. The room was

an island; the hallway, some childhoods. A memory

stood behind me, oddly tidy, I didn't catch its name.

Rows of us smelling like powder, sea-foam, eggshells.

The room was neither in front nor behind me, though

when I thought I saw an egret, I tore my doubts

into palatable samples and tossed them into the conditioned air.

We ate handsomely. There was enough to drink, the sky

having been tucked in with more sea. The memory

to my left asked after Gustavo. The memory to my right needed

Salomé. Over my shrinking feet, shells resembling brains.

The memory of the room was another island altogether, but

when the hallway widened, I happily mistook it for the world.

CENTERPIECE

Your condition: *suddenly* then *permanently*.

Long-stemmed sympathy flowers making the short-stemmed sympathy flowers
  look pathetic.

Like the feeding tube, your body swallowed its spiders.

Psalms on your phone bordered by orange advertisements, afterwards, late
  morning.

My suspicion: G-d is for playing G-d, looking away.

My evidence: Your blood accepting other blood product in a ward with light
  pink curtains.

Muscles at the front of the thigh, muscles that lift the front of the foot—
  they lack empathy.

If I lie for you, Mother, I'll feel it the most.

ARS POETICA

You skewer
all the present moments

with a fork. They squirm
spectacularly, like second languages.

A fate—
can you stomach it?

Anyway, you eat it. You eat it anyway.

AT THE CENTER OF THE STORY & UTTERLY LEFT OUT

Para Elena Milagro de Hoyos (1909–1931)

"I"-thoughts—
all any of us have.

I'm having the thought *it's too late*
in my life to stop crying.

Elena
can we practice this?

I notice I'm having the thought
it's too late in my life to stop crying.

There are things beyond
belief, like garlic, like

we have the same wrists.
How
did you place yours when you sang, sweetly?

.

Elena
yesterday I saw the reddest fire hydrant
imaginable.

It wasn't beyond belief, but I was
startled.

That kind of red should only exist
inside of us, I think.

I wish neither of us could recognize that
color.

.

Do you believe we want enough of ourselves?

Once a week I walk to the same construction site
a mile away from my home.

I kick one rock out of formation
from a larger pile of rocks.

No one sees me. No men have punished me.

Elena
I'm saying no men have punished me because of these walks.

.

Rudolph Valentino.
Did you know he was nearsighted?

Elena
your favorite actor was nearsighted.

I feel quite unreal
he said once, maybe twice
into a beautiful microphone.

You and I
the difference between us

I look severe,
I don't like having my picture taken, I just don't.

.

I had
the nightmare again

about choking on a bay leaf,
real fear like girls are real.

In real life, it happens most
when someone else has served you.

Elena
on accident and not,
when have you ignored the dangers?

Elena
Elena
they were wrong

Elena

our mothers were wrong about kindness

SACRIFICIAL MEAL

I

The recipe calls for 1 can of evaporated milk,
1 can of condensed milk, and ½ cup of whole milk.
The weather forecast calls for guayaberas and setting your country ablaze.
I am all out of sugar.

II

It takes a special kind of technician to handle a wildfire,
a certain type of person to forget the baking powder.
You retreated with a prehistoric determination.
I stopped anticipating needs and set the table for one.
I am an excellent conductor of heat.

III

Remember when I taught you how to alternate the milk?
I spoke to you in Spanish, like that movie about cooking
that didn't even get nominated. Everything a generic substitute
for desire, I rolled my *r*'s like phyllo dough.

IV

These days, I swell with small victories:
I sliced my finger while cutting tomatoes, though not to the bone.
I stopped naming the onions. I cry a little less.

V

In the movie, Tita is madly in love with her sister's husband, Pedro.
When her sister dies, they make passionate love.
Pedro dies mid-orgasm, so Tita swallows
a pair of matches and burns down the family ranch.
Anything, I mean anything, can triple in volume.

SONNET WITH OGUN

Plátanos frying in a cast-iron skillet. Wind

gone wrong, gone-gone the tamarind tree

from the overgrown easement. I've aged. Once,

a Yanqui lover tried to make me tostones. He didn't

know you have to fry them twice, a show of muscle

in between. Now, I brandish a plate that is not mine

from a cupboard that is not mine in a house I no longer live in.

Men working on the neighbor's renovation play

the same song on repeat from a small, silver boom box

though their hammering eclipses all other sound.

At the dinner table, I am told science

no longer recognizes the shape of my father's spine.

Later, when I clean the kitchen, I drop a knife on the floor

again and again just as an excuse to touch it.

ATTACHMENT THEORY

Ponce de León was a comemierda.

Picasso, too.

And your raiders, where do you keep their heads?

In the next room, a cockroach trapped and hardening.

I adjust the showerhead as if turning the face of my lover.

What am I trying to prove? I hate the ocean, I doubt my instincts.

The year I let a man watch me eat, my hair lifted
        off my head like a seat cover.

ABSOLUTE TRUTH

Wild rabbits steering clear of the yard.
If I were anyone else—
a thought I don't complete.

The lamp in the very next room,
and the first time I'd say *No*.
I spent the next day cooking.

I didn't have enough Tupperware
for what you'd done. In the evening,
an exorbitant amount of time

trying to decide which side of the glass
the bug was on—the reflection
of its splittable legs on the light linen curtain.

Shame: the top of my face, less skin.

NATURE & NURTURE, MIAMI, FL

Then restlessness. A hole in the roof and ceiling, quite numbing,
    smelling like peppercorns.

Your mother is unable to swallow, close her eyes fully when resting,
    consider death.

Now I am going to tell you this, you say aloud, suffering.

For years you bucketed your bathwater, your dishwater; they called you a petulant
    child then used the buckets to flush the toilets bloated with shit and piss.

The assumption behind most questions: you do want to live, don't you?

Heat humiliates; the lack of A/C is neon.

A feral colony of Florida honeybees settles in the hole in the roof and ceiling.
    Less numbing, somehow.

As punishment for withholding, you are made to sit in a black leather chair
    facing a wall of coquina rock. You have permission to cry but not to use
    the bathroom. To overachieve but not to slouch.

You are unmoved to learn that most parents do not successfully transmit
    their political values onto their children.

So you must ask for help when unscrewing it, the lid on your brain tightens.

Your father asks: *You do want to live, don't you?*

Only you are horrified when the mother possum falls like spit from the hole
    in the roof and ceiling, collecting rainwater, unexplained.

BINGE / FUGUE

Light like the veins of horses,
a familiar silence.

Have you ever overflowed? Haven't you?

First, they caught his scent. Rat-sweet, *like raisins steeped in urine*, said the bank teller. Then, a description: *brutish, unnatural, a chin so split it could snag a breeze.* Not two miles from the crime scene, he surrenders in every language he knows, three Glock 23's trained to his temples. He doesn't write to us until his fourth year but when he does, he only wants to talk about the yard. *Prima, I run around in circles como un perro.* I imagine a dizzying orange. His voice a leaking tub, he trades bruises the size of hand fruits with the boys on his block, says he can trick the unspooling of his gums into tasting like picadillo. I am trite, useless, when I visit his mother. We sit and silence. Then, *I found this in his room while cleaning—can you believe it? After all this time?* A note in her left palm, twitching:

MY MANIFESTO
Money is a small room
then, stairs.

Ascend.

SONNET FOR OBATALÁ

My head is yours. The amount of its heaven,

its lightness under any given thoughtspell.

The rest of me too—the little I love of living

folded behind my knees—Padre, I can feel it

weathering. Today I am the same age Goethe was

when he fell in love with a woman's bruised eye.

She saw white where there wasn't and then everything

became fraught with shine. Tell me, was she to argue

with light? This all started with a hen spreading dirt

atop the sea—we take shape because the continents

need swelt. It is nice to be needed. Wanted,

though that is its own suffering. In the evening, I learn

a fox can hear a clock ticking from forty yards away.

I am so endable, and yet, I am kept.

SELF-DETERMINATION THEORY

"There is something in this native land
business and you cannot get away from it."
—GERTRUDE STEIN

I sit in the living room,
in the living room
my mother chokes
on something cold and sharp.
I launch an investigation:
She is wearing a blue cotton shirt.
Her shoulders are showing.
The television is hush.
I conclude she is struggling
with a unique idea.
One she should keep.
Just like that, sparks. Reds,
whites. It is the savior
Mother calls US!
US places
his arms around her abdomen
and applies sudden
upward pressure. She heaves.
The volume
of the not-news channel
rises, and the sound alerts
my father in the kitchen.
To enter the living room,
my father must
step over the bodies of
other Spanish-speaking men.

He does so with ease.
I weep in the living room,
in the living room
my father watches US
grope my mother,
and though he is a jealous man,
he says nothing
because he, too,
accepts no other touch.

PLACE / SETTINGS

From the other end of the table, where are you sitting in these poems?

Neatly atop the cloth napkin.

From the head of the table, where are you sitting in these poems?

Underneath the placemat, wriggling.

From my mind that does not know, where are you sitting in these poems?

To the right of the knife.

From my heart that cannot know, where are you sitting in these poems?

In the tabletop glue joints.

From my gut that needs to know, where are you sitting in these poems?

I have fastened them around me like bibs.

WILL THE LAST AMERICAN TO LEAVE MIAMI PLEASE BRING THE FLAG?

Roaches on the ceiling—even they don't want to walk
where we walk

Dead brain
twitch
begging for it

NPR says the city has rented refrigerated container trucks
to store the overflow of bodies

The officer asks to see our legs
in the air, a struggle

When something of mine breaks
or we bruise from impact—

That's G-d.

SONNET WITH ORULA

At my fourth consulta the Babalawo says he will recover

and she will not. My eyeline greens. I lean like a shovel,

lower as a handprint. This is a daughter's future, plural,

legible only in the script of another. The back of my neck

peeling in sheets thin enough to dissolve on a tongue.

I am to spend more time in tall grass, watching

the cycle of bugs. I am to spend more time cradling weight

in my palms, especially fruit that hides its rot. White smoke

waves the room. I say thank you in a language I used to cover

my eyes before speaking. Blessings and energy. Iré and aché.

On the drive home, a cast of pregnant land crabs

scuttle across the road at the request of the moon. I know

the moon does not think me important. The stars could be

showing me their backs, and I couldn't do a thing about it.

PROPAGANDA GHAZAL

Father repeats a Yanqui saying about History, its wrong side.
In fear of comeuppance, I eat so much I can only sleep on my side.

For years I thought our guts looked like unupholstered chairs.
That this unlearning would be a larger spectacle, a bright side.

America, Wake Up, the bazooka blasts are cartoon tomatoes.
I line up the lies like handholding children—side by side by side.

FIDEL CASTRO *is a threat to the peace of the Western Hemisphere!*
For an eye-catching poster, use the color wheel's opposite sides.

I didn't fuck the woman with the Che Guevara print above her
bed. Instead, I let her pin new atrocities to my damp, right side.

MASSIVE ACTIVITY

US MEANING SUFFERING OR DISEASE

****

If they die.
Ticks gently ██████████████ like mother's kisses.

US man cradles a new canister inside a new aircraft.
He is the size of a pathogen from where they stand.

They die.
He is the size of a pathogen from where they lie.

****

US START RUMORS (MANY)

****

It is most important that an impression is given.

Say: FIDEL is only concerned with his cock and belly—neck-down living.
Imagine: grand table trimmings in a grand hall in a grand residence, lavish women
   eating lavishly.

The ███████████ won't know the difference between a real and fake photograph.

Say: they couldn't possibly know the difference.

****

US SINK A BOATLOAD OF ███████████████████ (REAL OR
SIMULATED)

****

The impact must be real enough to change the color of water
and simulated enough to change the color of water and hide it
       from the news.

Hold steady to the belief that we are making right.
That we are administering justice given our actions
       to make, to do.

****

US SAY THIS ON HIGHER AUTHORITY

****

TOP SECRET ██████████

Higher Authority is ██████████ *progress* . . .

Higher Authority ██████████████ *is not* ██████████ *time* . . .

Higher Authority ██████████████ *would* ██████████ *come from within* . . .

Higher Authority ██████████████ *will be made* ████████████████

████████████████ ONLY

****

US ESPECIALLY IN THE SABOTAGE FIELD
****

We believe there is a field where their people rest without US.
Magnolia trees, serpentine rocks, warm dogs, warm lizards,
███████, dry feet.

We believe the island is subservient to the dreams of the island.

So wake them up. So put them down again.
****

US RETAIN A LOW NOISE LEVEL
****
(This is not possible.)
****

US ███████████ WOULD BE BLAMED ON THE UNITED STATES
****
If they die, it is most important that an impression is given.

The impact must be real enough to change the color of water,
TOP SECRET ███████████.

We believe there is a field where their people rest without US.

(This is not possible.)

THREAT DISPLAY

*"Exploding a few plastic bombs in carefully chosen spots,
the arrest of Cuban agents and the release of prepared
documents substantiating Cuban involvement also
would be helpful in projecting the idea of an irresponsible
government."*
—"JUSTIFICATION FOR US MILITARY INTERVENTION
IN CUBA (TS)," WASHINGTON, DC, 13 MARCH, 1962.

Unfastening
the smallest bones

of the rebellion.

Auditory snow:

    A kick to the head
that misses.

(*Sana, sana, culita de rana*)

Does the spic cover
their ears long after?

    .

Blood woofer.

Counterintelligent.

A specter
in the vestibule—

Bolshevik?—

A check
of the exits.

.

In utero,
the ear develops

on the lower neck
before moving

upward.

More scraping
of the sides,

more sliding.

.

You could fit
a brain

in a bass drum,
a snare drum,

a floor tom.

You could
hold it

up like a boom.

THREAT DISPLAY

2017: President Trump accuses Cuba of employing sonic attacks against the employees of the US embassy in Cuba. The Cuban government denies any wrongdoing.

What to discontinue?

Indecent crickets—
native—
all stages, times of year?

People
and their
      suddenness!

You think above-
ground, above
sea,
eyes and ears.

You think device,
small,
every corner, more.

We are sorry

for the way we talk
      in English,

but The Scientists
are not sorry.

They have emptied
the air for you!

Made blank the soil!

You must know—
The Republic

          only minds

The Republic.

So now we give
you our word—

your words back.
We give you
a shovel.

Bury one only.

THREAT DISPLAY

Lo siento, no podemos
responder a ninguna pregunta.

No vivimos aquí,
solo sobrevivimos aquí.

It takes many anniversaries to reach the diamond anniversary in which the modern appropriate gift is diamonds, and screams can be heard inside and outside of the coercer and target. You are cordially invited to 1991, please visit with your US dollar. Chant it with me now—pressure, undermine, replace! President Kennedy, MAXIMUM LEADER, though we are starved we have sent the goat into the wilderness as asked, soiled with sugar, nickel, citrus. An effective alternative to military intervention is economic strangulation, a compression of the blood vessels, so says. *In the #Havana destination, our hotels are operating normally.* Simultaneous "Hand over that Cold War Nostalgia, President Clinton," and, it is more human than this. A shaving of animal fat the family can chew on from both ends is a prime example of horizontal integration. Circle the irony: President Reagan accuses financeless country of financing terrorism. Did you read "human" and think callous? Angel of meaningful democratic changes asks that you connect your Facebook page to your WhatsApp before posting: *Used oxygen tank available for trade, need children's ibuprofen.* As for vertical integration, they are producing tears that can move bottom to top, rapidly, their most plentiful export. By decree, we, the Cuban Americans, claim a monopoly on smithereens.

LIBRETA DE ABASTECIMIENTO

Food rationing supply book

No grazing a dead acre.

No stretching the unfit,

No flour,

No four-legged wealth wobbling to pasture.

No empathy spell.

No grease slab, no hatchlings,

No dairy,

No intact hard palate.

No rot liability.

No armfuls, no alchemy,

No hope kernel,

No furnace.

No brightening fuel.

No delicacy.

No phantom taste,

No in bloom,

No tender,

No water,

No after,

No ice.

FAILED STATE / FALSE IMAGES

July 11–17, 2021

What men call dead called missing,
calls to combat announced
like dinner plans.
With their oversized helmet visors,
the dictator's special forces
resemble EpiPens.
Cuba is deeply allergic to hatred, says the dictator.

A photojournalist's left eye
is outstripped
by Revolutionary National Police.
His left eye is left
absent by its own
skin, in its place the wet
red of sinked raspberries.
In the little Soviet refrigerators,
no fruits,
no raspberries.

To hold a sign like ABAJO LA DICTADURA
PATRIA Y VIDA
above your head
requires you to round your arms,
become more circular.
It requires constant speed.
When the demonstrators link hands

they, like lack, become circular,
rolling on and on and
on and on
like blackouts.

The Black Wasps wear green berets,
the Prevention Troops wear red berets,
and the Revolutionary National Police wear black berets.
The group of men that broke
into the house
of the missing man
and fired
behind his head
wore black berets.

Where are the Cuban murders? asks the dictator. *Where
are the disappeared in Cuba?*

The blood of the minors
who throw small rocks
at state security vehicles
does not flow in the streets of Havana,
Santiago de Cuba,
Santa Clara,
Ciego de Ávila,
Camagüey,
Guantánamo,
San José de las Lajas,
Cárdenas, y más,
but in their precincts.

Irrefutable, a young mother
in a pink disposable face mask
waits in line for eight days
to fill her car with diesel.
The little food in her
Soviet refrigerator rots.
All around her, the detained
clang their handcuffs
against the backs of their skulls
as if scoring the coming
of eternity.

MALECÓN / MIAMI

*"Cuban experts say Havana's boardwalk
could be underwater by 2100."*
—THE DAILY MAIL

*"Many of Miami Beach's landmarks,
the world famous South Beach, and the
picturesque art deco hotels of Ocean Drive,
will be lost within three decades."*
—THE GUARDIAN

So, the ocean refused to stay a tourist.
So, G-d doesn't give with both hands.

We are wading in as little clothing as crabs,
brown bags,
brown bags with liquor in our wet hands.

Who could save the this in us?

More than once, we swam around dying
for a minute. A look to the heavens, spent,

sound of a crash, a currency, a beating.

We will miss what did not belong to us,
yes.

In wake of our absence, we submit
wallets of breath to the ocean floor.

SONNET FOR OCHÚN

After my left arm I washed my right, neck, décolletage,

and navel. I ate ground meat with large crystals of imported salt.

The women and men who would stroke my hair if I asked,

I thought of them fondly then sadly. At the flea market,

what I touched with a fingernail was a copper lamp, a mundane

painting of mountains, the cashier's hum. I bought nothing I didn't

want. In the cul-de-sac, I found clouds on leashes, loose roosters.

I thought thoughts ugly as clothespins. Reading a used book,

I suspected I knew less about death than the last person who held it.

I spat into a mirrored sink. I lost my slippers and face. To feel more

like water, I drank it. Before bed, I walked my plank of uncertainties

and plunged further into uncertainty. *Am I capturing all of history*

in this gesture? I shouted into the future. In the wet air of the future,

I could have but never appeared. No one was sorry but me.

REMEDIOS

Para Mamacita

When G-d was a boy the dirt was dark red
and the myths of women, explicit.
Just enough of the world had been distributed
to know what was possible—what you didn't,
couldn't, have. Love hid in the kernels
of handsome mamey fruit. We sorted
through piles of black beans in case they lied
about its whereabouts, we built ladders
we were too tired to climb. We cried.
Eventually, we cried so often we were forced
to invent salvation. We'd fill the largest bucket
we could find with the coldest water. We'd
sit the crier down and crowd behind her.
After several synchronized breaths, we'd lift
the bucket and tip it downward. What was left
no longer resembled crying, but we chanted
come back, come back to us, anyway.

NOTES

This book takes its title from the following passage in Hemingway's *The Old Man and the Sea*: "Eat it so that the point of the hook goes into your heart and kills you, he thought. Come up easy and let me put the harpoon into you. All right. Are you ready? Have you been long enough at table?"

"Bodied, or Day 1 of 9" references the nine days of national mourning decreed by the Cuban government following the death of Fidel Castro.

"A Story of Love & Faith / La Milagrosa" references the legend of Amelia Goyri de la Hoz, who is considered an unofficial saint of Cuba. The cemetery referenced in this poem is La Necrópolis de Cristóbal Colón in Havana. This poem also alludes to Cuban sculptor José Vilalta Saavedra.

"Apostle" is for José Martí. The line *"Amor cuerdo, no es amor"* comes from his poem "Dolora griega."

"Miguelito / Marielito" takes inspiration from Simone Lueck's photographs of televisions inside Cuban homes.

"Glassware" references a 1964 *New York Times* article titled "HAVANA ACCLAIMS BOY CANE-CUTTER; Asserts 12-Year-Old Cuts 7,608 Pounds a Day."

"Left Arm / Right Arm" is inspired by Ana Mendieta's 1974 performance art piece "Body Tracks (Rastros Corporales): Blood Sign #2."

The italicized Spanish words in "Gusano" are taken from Fidel Castro's famous speech on January 2, 1961, in which he celebrated the two-year anniversary of the revolution and denounced counterrevolutionaries and their children as worms, privileged, terrorists, parasites, and cowards.

"Operation Good Times" takes its title from an Anti-Castro CIA plan that involved disseminating a fake photo of an obese Fidel Castro lording over a banquet of food with lavish women draped over him. The caption was to read "My ration is different."

The phrase "At the Center of the Story & Utterly Left Out" appears in episode 610 of the podcast *This American Life*. My poem of the same name owes a great debt to Jean Valentine's "Lucy" sequence from her book *Break the Glass*. Most importantly, this poem is dedicated to Elena Milagro de Hoyos. May she be remembered for her humanity.

"Sacrificial Meal" interacts in part with the 1992 Mexican film *Como agua para chocolate*.

The epigraph that appears before "Self-Determination Theory" is borrowed from Gertrude Stein's *Wars I Have Seen*.

"Will the Last American to Leave Miami Please Bring the Flag?" takes its title from a racist 1980s bumper sticker that populated South Florida following the Mariel boatlift, in which hundreds of thousands of Cubans and Haitians sought asylum in the United States. While the Cuban immigrants were considered political refugees, the Haitian immigrants were considered "economic migrants" and did not receive the same protections.

"Massive Activity" engages with real and manipulated text from declassified documents that outline Operation Mongoose and Operation Northwoods—two covert projects masterminded by the Pentagon that sought to incite a counter-revolution and/or assassinate Fidel Castro, and justify a US invasion of Cuba via scapegoat terrorism, respectively. Language in the first section of this poem is inspired by Lorca's poem "Farewell," translated by W. S. Merwin. The details of Operation Good Times are referenced in section two.

The complete attribution for the epigraph that appears before "Threat Display ['Unfastening']" is: "Justification for US Military Intervention in Cuba (TS)" from "Annex to Appendix to Enclosure A," in L.L. Lemnitzer, Chairman, Joint Chiefs of Staff "Memorandum for the Secretary of Defense," Washington, DC, 13 March, 1962.

"Threat Display ['*Lo siento, no podemos*']" borrows a quote from the 2017 *Miami Herald* article "While tourists drink water out of a bottle, Cubans ration and boil a limited supply."

In "Context Eternal," the line "In the #Havana destination, our hotels are operating normally" is lifted from a tweet by the Gaviota Turismo-Cuba's Twitter account, dated 9/29/2022. Hurricane Ian devastated the island on 9/26/2022, and the majority of the island's citizens did not have power on 9/29/2022.

"Failed State / False Images" takes its title from separate remarks given by US President Joe Biden and Cuban President Miguel Díaz-Canel in reaction to the July 2021 protests in Cuba. Joe Biden called Cuba a "failed state" that is "repressing" its citizens. Miguel Díaz-Canel was quoted saying "What the world is seeing of Cuba is a lie," and decried the sharing of "false images" on social media.

The epigraphs that appear before "Malecón / Miami" are lifted from an article in *The Daily Mail* dated November 1, 2017, and titled "Havana's top tourist attraction threatened by climate change: The Malecon boulevard could be underwater by 2100, say experts"; and an article in *The Guardian* dated April 21, 2020, and titled "Will Florida be lost forever to the climate crisis?"

"Remedios" is named after a small Cuban town in the former province of Las Villas where my beloved grandmother, Beatriz, was born.

ACKNOWLEDGMENTS

This book was made possible by the generous and affirming support of Carnegie Mellon University, the University of Wisconsin-Madison Creative Writing MFA program, CantoMundo, the Stadler Center for Poetry & Literary Arts, and the National Endowment for the Arts.

Thank you to my angel, Jan Verberkmoes, for being the person I, and by extension, these poems, could always count on.

Thank you to Marci Calabretta Cancio-Bello for knowing what I needed before I even thought to ask, in life and in this work.

Thank you to Alisha Dietzman for emboldening me every step of the way, and for your influence and sisterhood.

Gratitude unbound to my teachers, mentors, workshop instructors, and those who gave early support: Terrance Hayes, Jim Daniels, Gerald Costanzo, Sean Bishop, Jesse Lee Kercheval, Amy Quan Barry, Amaud Jamal Johnson, G. C. Waldrep, Ilya Kaminsky, Ada Limón, Daniel Borzutzky, Richard Blanco, Zeina Hashem Beck, and Victoria Chang.

All my love to the unrivaled team at Tin House, including Beth Steidle, Becky Kraemer, Nanci McCloskey, Jae Nichelle, Craig Popelars, David Caligiuri, and Nicole Pagliari. To my superb editor, Alyssa Ogi, thank you for talking me down from every ledge, and for creating the conditions in which I could do my best work. Thank you to Elizabeth DeMeo for opening the door.

For the encouragement, check-ins, and keen insights: Carolyn Orosz, K. A. Hays, Sean Patrick Mulroy, Sophie Klahr, Aurora Masum-Javed, Carly Joy Miller, Ricky Maldonado, Lindsey Alexander, Eric Kocher, John Allen Taylor, and Josh Kalscheur.

To my extraordinary family, earthly and divine: my mother, Salomé, my father Gustavo, my brother, Nicholas—your love sustains me. To Mamacita, whose spirit I try to honor in everything I do.

To my partner, Lee Holden, for loving me so fiercely and patiently. I adore you.

To my cats, Julius and Chowder, for stressing the importance of rest, boundaries, and play. You saved my life.

I am indebted to the editors and reading staff of the following journals for taking a chance on these poems, oftentimes in their infancy:

jubilat: "Ño"

Ninth Letter: "Sonnet for Eleguá," "Sonnet with Ogun"

Hayden's Ferry Review: "Bodied, or Day 1 of 9"

The Adroit Journal: "A Story of Love & Faith / La Milagrosa,"
"Gusano," "Centerpiece," "Sonnet with Orula"

Four Way Review: "Sunday, Wounded"

Southern Indiana Review: "Climate Feedback"

Post Road: "Miguelito / Marielito"

The Florida Review: "Sierra del Escambray"

Narrative: "Sonnet for Shango"

Gravy Quarterly: "Still Life with Christ, Aromatics"

AGNI: "Mal de Ojo," "Sonnet for Obatalá"

POOL: "Sacrificial Meal"

Yale Review: "Absolute Truth"

Black Warrior Review: "Case #901200530"

New England Review: "Self-Determination Theory," "Propaganda Ghazal"

Memorious: "Libreta de Abastecimiento," "Malecón / Miami"

Poem-a-Day: "Sonnet for Ochún"

Kenyon Review: "Remedios"

Early versions of "Will the Last American to Leave Miami Please Bring the Flag" and "Threat Display ['Unfastening']" appeared in the anthology *Até Mais: Latinx Futurisms* published by Deep Vellum Publishing.

© HILLARY DUBIE

LESLIE SAINZ is the recipient of a 2021 National Endowment for the Arts Poetry Fellowship. Her work has appeared in the Academy of American Poets' *Poem-a-Day*, *Yale Review*, *Kenyon Review*, *AGNI*, *Narrative*, and elsewhere. A three-time National Poetry Series finalist, she's received scholarships, fellowships, and honors from CantoMundo, The Miami Writers Institute, *The Adroit Journal*, and The Stadler Center for Poetry & Literary Arts at Bucknell University. The daughter of Cuban exiles, she is originally from Miami, Florida, and lives in Vermont, where she is the managing editor of the *New England Review*.